The Chicken Wings Cookbook

Featuring Appetizing Recipes You Will Like

By

Angel Burns

License Notices

This book or parts thereof might not be reproduced in any format for personal or commercial use without the written permission of the author. Possession and distribution of this book by any means without said permission is prohibited by law.

All content is for entertainment purposes and the author accepts no responsibility for any damages, commercially or personally, caused by following the content.

Table of Contents

Introduction

The appeal of wings has increased a great deal among consumers. With the aid of several varieties launched in various restaurants, consumers can achieve the highest price of any kind of wings. It is certainly recommended that you eat it in moderation so that it will not cause havoc in your stomach.

Chicken wings have become very popular with so many flavors and textures. It's very easy to plan, and in just a limited time, you can add something to the party menu in a very short time. They are available in several markets, and they also sell various parts individually so that you can find your favorite one. There is a huge quantity of meat available in this section, which is why the customers are so demanding. The middle portion of the wing is known as flat because of its shape, so it does not contain dark meat. Indeed, the feathery shape at the end of the wing is known as tips and contains so little beef, but it also tastes like chicken wings, and people enjoy it.

Chicken wings have become the food that many people judge a bar/restaurant by. Many establishments don't list them in the appetizer area of the menu anymore but have given them their own section. This dish has somehow risen above the starter's caste. We are huge fans of chicken wings. So huge, we even have a dedicated website and blog about them. The wing, whether you refer to it as a hot wing, buffalo wing, or chicken wing, is a new food which is funny in and of itself because humans have been raising the chicken and eating that delicious bugger for a long time. Sure, people have been eating chicken wings as long as they've been eating chickens, but the actual, official, original buffalo wing didn't hit the scene until 1964.

It's a nice story, and does our heart good to see this establishment is still in business and that you can actually order wings from them on the internet.

After a stressful day at work, all you need to do is take a bite of a tasty, tender steak, juicy, delicious chicken wings that are slow-cooked to perfection. So, when you get the shot, you immediately feel relaxed so fulfilled. Are there any vegetarians? My apologies.

For example, if you've grown up thinking about chicken wing-based food as a source of warmth and happiness, it will affect you tremendously.

Every traditional comfort food has chicken wings in it. And, for many people, eating these meals will make them happy, more relaxed, or more excited. The dietitian in me does not want to ignore the idea of a personal relationship with food, simply because each person has one.

There is literally an increasing number of people in the world who are interested in Chicken Wing recipes. Indeed, there is usually an increase in the price of chicken wings whenever there is a super bowl. It is estimated that at super bowls weekends, fans may consume up to 1.38 billion chicken wings. This fact shows how much value that is ascribed to the chicken wing. As of the year 2019, the prices of chicken wings soared even higher. If you really love chicken wings, then this is the recipe book you should take a look at.

This book covers simple chicken wing recipes like; Cola Chicken wings, Fried Garlicky Wings, Classic Honey-Soy Wings, and many more. If you are concerned about making recipes that require the removal of bone from chicken nibbles, then you should rest undoubtedly that this is the book for you. This book also gives detailed steps on how to debone chicken nibbles. You are likely to come across measuring units like; Grams, Kilograms, Liter, and so on.

Some of the equipment which is needed alongside a clear copy of this recipe book is Saucepan, Fry pan, Wok, Spatula, Air fryer, or deep fryer.

The difficulty level of each recipe is shallow, and this means that everyone will be able to make all the recipes in this book. These recipes employ the use of common ingredients like, Bamboo leaves, Bay leaf, Coconut oil, Coconut Cream, Chicken stock, Palm sugar, Soybean paste, Rice vinegar, White sesame seed, Fish sauce, Dried chili, and a few others. These ingredients are widespread, and you can get them from any supermarket. The duration it takes to complete each of the recipes in this book is also concise, and hence, you get to satisfy yourself within a very short period.

It is essential to get the exact steps it takes to make the recipes, and this is why this book has been literally written to carefully guide you through all the steps necessary to reach the peak of satisfaction.

On game days, they're all expecting the latest chicken wings. We've got all the hints and tricks for the golden brown delicacies.

Step One: Remove tips of the wing

Usually, when you buy chicken wings, you get the entire wing, which has three sections: the middle, the wingette, and the drumette. Although I might be called to clipping (forgive me a soccer pun), there is so little meat in the tip, and it burns quickly, and I like to cut the bit and conserve it to make a stock or a broth. Using a sharp, slender knife, slash through the joint between the tip of the wing and the winglet. If you move the joints, it's going to be easy to see precisely where to chop.

Step two: Separate wingette and drumet

Move the joint between the wingette and the drumette should teach you just where to cut and split it. Test Kitchen tip: if you want to skip the first two steps, you can purchase frozen and thawed wingettes or drumettes. We're not going to tell.

Step Three: Chill

Salting and cooling can dry the skin slightly, which is the trick to making the skin crisp when it is fried. Just be sure to put them uncovered in the refrigerator to dissolve the moisture.

Step Four: Fry it up!

A deep fryer at home is awesome for cooking wings, but you do not need to worry if you do not have one. The electric stove fits well, or you can substitute with a Dutch oven on the stovetop. Fill it with oil enough that when the wings are applied, there should be at least one inch of oil filled with no risk of bubbling over the rim.

Step Five: Prepare the sauce

Now is your chance to be innovative and simply throw your fried wings with one of the sauces.

How to Cook Chicken Wings

1. Air-Fryer Chicken Wings

You should use your air fryer to get crisp wings with no excess oil. Spray the interior of your cooking spray air fryer container and place the wings with a gap between them so that they can possibly be crisp. Don't want to hurry stuff by frying the whole batch at once, or else the wings won't be crisp. Give this Buffalo Chicken Wings Air Fryer a try.

2. Baked Chicken Wings

The trick to having crispy baked wings is the use of baking strength in the coating. These Crispy Honey Sriracha Chicken Wings are going to show you the way.

3. Grilled Chicken Wings

Yeah, the wings are fantastic on the grill. Commonly, the grilled wings have a milder sauce, because the smoky, caramelized taste of the flames is the star. When you're in love with your BBQ, the Grill expert Chicken Wings is for you.

4. Instant Pot Chicken Wings

With this procedure, you don't need to defrost the frozen chicken wings until you cook them in a 2-step cycle that begins in your Instant Pot and finishes with a fast crisp under the broiler. This Instant Pot Crispy Chicken Wings recipe gives you step-by-step guidance.

5. Fried Chicken Wings

If you just need classic chicken wings, seasoned and fried to crushing crusty perfection, try the Buffalo Chicken Wings dining-Style.

6. Slow Cooker Chicken Wings

It's quick, hands-off, and it's all cooked in one pan, so it's fast from start to finish. Was a larger party scheduled for you? Start setting up the super slow cookers for the Incredible Slow Cooker Buffalo Wings.

Chicken Wings Recipe

Chicken Wings are the go-to favorite food of everyone. The following are 50+ different recipes that you can do to level up your chicken wing dish. From the sourest, to the sweetest, to the spiciest, to the saltiest, and many more!

Summer's Sweet and Sour Chicken Wings

Satisfy everyone with these cooked chicken wings as an appetizer; their sweet honey glaze is balanced with soy sauce and vinegar. Garlic and ginger give a welcome blow, lifting wings to the game-day territory.

Servings: 8

Cook time: 45 minutes

Ingredients:

- 2 ½ lb. Chicken Wings
- 1/3 C. Cooking Oil (Possibly More)
- 1/3 C. Vinegar
- 1/2 C. Packed Dark Brown Sugar
- 1 (12 oz.) Can Unsweetened Pineapple Juice
- ¾ c. Ketchup
- 1 tbsp. Soy Sauce
- 1 tsp. Prepared Mustard
- 1/8 tsp. Salt (Optional)

Instructions:

1. Heat the oil on stove in a good size deep saucepan. Use caution while heating oil and when cooking wings in hot oil, especially when first adding them to the oil.

2. Brown wings in hot oil, adding more oil if necessary.

3. Next, remove wings from oil as they brown and place on towel paper-lined plate to drain additional oil from wings.

4. Using a second good size deep saucepan, add vinegar, sugar, pineapple juice, ketchup, soy sauce, mustard, and salt to saucepan. Bring to a steady simmer, stirring occasionally.

5. Simmer gently for about 5 minutes, remembering to stir.

6. Add browned chicken wings to the sauce.

7. Next, cover the saucepan and simmer on low for about 15 minutes.

8. Cook for another 15 minutes.

9. Remove from your oven and let sit a few minutes then use tongs to move from pan to serving plate.

Honey and Soy Sauce Chicken Wings

Really yummy and simple chicken wings made with honey and soy sauce in the oven. Quick and easy daily meal!

Servings: 6

Cook time: 6-7 hours

Ingredients:

- 1 tsp. chili powder
- 20 chicken wings
- 1 c. soy sauce
- 1 c. honey
- 2 c. brown sugar
- 1 tsp. lemon juice
- 1 tsp. Worcestershire sauce
- 1 tsp. ground ginger
- 1 tsp. salt
- 1 tsp. pepper

Instructions:

1. In your mixing bowl, mix together everything except the chicken wings.

2. Put half of the mixture into the slow cooker.

3. Add the chicken wings in the slow cooker and cover with the rest of the sauce.

4. Cook on low for 6 - 7 hours.

Honey Flavored Chicken Wings

Honey's chicken wings are simply divine. They're soft and spicy, and they're the best complement to any bowl. These wings are baked to crispiness and tossed with a honey garlic sauce.

Servings: 4

Cook time: 6-7 hours

Ingredients:

- 20 chicken wings
- 1 tsp. salt
- 1 tsp. pepper
- 1 ½ c. honey
- ½ c. soy sauce
- 3 tsp. ketchup
- ¼ c. brown sugar
- 1 garlic clove, minced

Instructions:

1. Add flavor to the chicken wings by sprinkling them with salt and pepper and place in slow cooker.

2. In another bowl, add together the honey, soy sauce, ketchup, garlic and brown sugar.

3. Once mixed, pour over chicken and mix well in order to ensure all the chickens are with coat.

4. Cook on low for 6 - 7 hours.

Crispy Mustard Chicken Wings

Chicken wings are flavored with a simple mixture of spices, then brushed with mustard and floured and fried to crisp... This chicken is so sweet!

Servings: 6

Cook time: 1 hour

Ingredients:

- 2 lb. Chicken Wings
- 2 tbsp. Mayonnaise
- 2 tbsp. Prepared Mustard
- ½ c. Dry Breadcrumbs
- ½ tsp. Dried Italian Seasoning
- Salt and Pepper to taste
- Cooking Oil to Grease Baking Pan

Instructions:

1. Preheat oven to 350 degrees.

2. Mix and stir the mayonnaise and mustard.

3. Toss the wings in the bowl that has your mustard/mayo mix. I use a spatula to help turn and coat the wings in the mixture.

4. Next, put the breadcrumbs and dried Italian seasoning in a gallon baggie. Add pepper and salt to taste and shake the bag well. (I use very little salt and some pepper. I use pink Himalayan salt and freshly ground pepper but you can use standard salt and pepper)

5. Add the coated wings to the baggie a few at a time. Shake well to coat each wing and place each coated wing in a greased baking pan.

6. Dredge in breadcrumb mixture.

7. Add the chicken in a 10 x 6 x 2 inch baking dish that has been coated with spray.

8. Next, cover loosely and bake at 350 degrees for 45 minutes.

9. Remove it and bake it again for 10-15 minutes or until chicken wings are thoroughly cooked.

10. Carefully remove hot pan from oven. Let pan sit for 3-5 minutes and then transfer wings to a serving platter.

Carnitas Chicken Wings

This recipe will show you the difference of Mexican dish to other chicken recipes.

Servings: 5

Cook time: 2-4 hours

Ingredients:

- 2 ½ lb. chicken drumettes, rinsed in cold water
- 2 tsp. salt
- 1/3 c. dried chile caribe
- 1 tsp. chipotle chile powder
- 1 onion, peeled and thinly sliced
- 8 cloves garlic, chopped
- 4 whole cloves, crushed
- 2 tsp. anise seeds
- 2 tsp. ground canella
- 2 tsp. oregano
- 1 bay leaf
- Zest and juice of 1 orange
- 2 tsp. brown sugar
- 2 c. chicken fat or duck fat

Instructions:

1. In a big bowl, mix the drumettes, salt, chile caribe, chile powder, onion, garlic, cloves, anise, canella, oregano, bay leaf, orange zest and juice, and sugar.

2. Toss to coat. Then, marinate in refrigerator for 2 hours.

3. Next, place the drumettes and chicken fat in a 6-quart slow cooker.

4. Cover drumettes with parchment paper, place lid on cooker, and cook on low for 3 hours. Remove slow cooker insert and let the wings cool at room temperature for 4 hours; refrigerate for 24 hours.

5. Next, heat a large nonstick frying pan to medium low, and remove as much of the fat as possible from the drumettes.

6. Fry on all sides, turning often. When the skin is golden, remove from the pan and serve with warm tortillas.

Speakeasy Apricot Wings

Simple cooked crispy chicken wings with a tasty light apricot glaze are the perfect game day snack and quick family dish.

Servings: 6

Cook time: 30 minutes

Ingredients:

- 3 lb. chicken wings
- 1 (10 oz.) jar apricot preserves
- 1 (8 oz.) bottle Creamy French Dressing
- 1 pkg. instant dry onion soup mix
- Cooking oil to brush wings

Instructions:

1. Preheat oven to 350 degree F.

2. Brush the wings lightly with cooking oil and bake in the oven for about 45 minutes to 60 minutes until thoroughly cooked.

3. While the wings are cooking - Heat apricot preserves and French dressing in a saucepan on low. Once the mix starts to simmer, thoroughly mix in the dry onion soup mix. Let the mix simmer on low 10-15 minutes, be sure to stir frequently.

4. Carefully remove the cooked wings and dip in the sauce. Place the wings back in the baking pan. If there is a lot of pan juice from baking wings, drain it out first before adding dipped wings.

5. Place pan of dipped wings back in oven for about 10 minutes.

6. Remove dipped wings from oven and using care transfer from hot baking pan to serving plate.

Diamond Jim's Bar Wings

This fried chicken wing is the best partner of beer.

Servings: 8

Cook time: 30 minutes

Ingredients:

- 3 lb. chicken wings
- ½ c. Buffalo wing sauce
- ½ c. barbecue sauce
- Cooking oil

Instructions:

1. Preheat oven to 350 degree F.

2. Grease pan.

3. Place wings in pan and brush lightly with oil.

4. Cover wings and bake at 350 for 45 minutes.

5. I always leave a small section of the cover open so my wings don't get soggy.

6. Mix the two sauces above together.

7. Remove wings and uncover – be very careful due to hot steam under cover.

8. Brush wings with the sauce combination and return to the oven uncovered.

9. In 5 to 7 minutes brush again and return to oven for 3-4 more minutes.

10. Remove from oven and brush wings again.

11. Then carefully move from baking pan to serving platter.

Guava & Chipotle Chicken Wings

Sweet & Hot Wings that are deliciously different.

Servings: 8

Cook time: 2 hours and 30 minutes

Ingredients:

- 3 lb. Chicken Wings
- ¾ c. Mayonnaise
- ¾ c. Guava Jelly
- 2 tbsp. Finely Chopped Chipotle Peppers In Adobo Sauce
- 2 tbsp. Dijon Mustard
- 1 Clove Garlic, Chopped
- Cooking Oil to Brush Wings

Instructions:

1. First, line the bottom of your broiler pan with aluminum foil.

2. Preheat oven to 425°F.

3. Lightly brush wings with cooking oil and place on broiler rack.

4. Bake for approximately 45 minutes.

5. While the wings are baking combine mayonnaise, guava jelly, chopped chipotle peppers, Dijon mustard and chopped garlic. Refrigerate the mixture.

6. Next, when 40-45 minutes have passed, you will carefully remove the wings from the oven.

7. Remove dip from refrigerator and put half in a separate bowl. Place the remaining half back in the fridge to use as a dip.

8. Brush the wings thoroughly with the mayo mixture. Place the wings on the rack and back in the oven for an additional 15 minutes. The wings will be golden brown and thoroughly cooked when done.

(You can also create this recipe on the grill versus oven).

9. Remove wings from heat using care. Place on serving platter and serve with the remaining mayo dip mixture.

Sticky Chinese Chicken Wings

These Chinese-style chicken wings will make a fancy dish at a dim sum party. But you can also prepare it anytime you wish when you crave for something sticky and yummy. It's a great treat for a family night, whether you are going to share it for dinner or over the movie.

Servings: 4

Cook time: 50 minutes

Ingredients:

- 2 lb. Chicken Wings, Separated into Wingettes And Drumettes
- 2 tbsp. Clementine Tangerine Juice
- 1 tbsp. Ginger, finely chopped
- 4 Garlic Cloves, Minced
- ¼ c. Soy Sauce
- 1 tbsp. Scallions, Finely Sliced
- 2 tbsp. Honey
- ½ tsp. Sesame Oil
- 2 tbsp. Mirin
- 2 tbsp. Oyster Sauce
- ¼ c. Tomato Paste
- 2 tbsp. Hoisin Sauce
- 1 tsp. Five-Spice Powder
- 2 tbsp. Sweet Chili Sauce
- ¼ tsp. Red Pepper Flakes, Crushed

Instructions:

1. Combine all in the bowl except for chicken wings and scallions, until well blended.

2. Transfer to a resealable plastic bag and add the chicken wings. Toss and massage to marinade evenly. Set aside in your fridge for 30 minutes to an hour.

3. Preheat the oven to 350 degrees F.

4. Put the parchment paper in the baking dish lined and add the chicken wings, saving the marinade for basting the meat.

5. Bake chicken wings for about 45 minutes, basting generously with the reserved marinade about twice or thrice during the cooking process.

6. Serve and enjoy.

Korean Chicken Wings

Here is a quick and easy chicken wing recipe that you will surely love. It's packed with Korean flavors that make it yummy in each bite. It's sticky because of the honey-based sauce and chunky because of toasted sesame seeds and the actual texture of the wings, which comes out crispy fried after treatment in hot oil.

Servings: 6

Cook time: 40 minutes

Ingredients:

- 1 ½ lb. Chicken Wings, Split and Patted Dry
- 2 tbsp. Sesame Seeds, Toasted
- 2 tbsp. Honey
- ¼ c. Sriracha
- ¼ c. Ketchup
- 1 tsp. Lemon Juice
- ½ c. Flour
- ½ c. Cornstarch
- 3 c. Vegetable Oil
- Kosher Salt and Ground Pepper to Taste

Instructions:

1. First, combine flour, cornstarch, salt, and pepper in a large bowl.

2. Toss chicken to coat evenly.

3. Heat oil over medium fire until the temperature reaches 350 degrees F.

4. Next, add chicken wings, shaking off excess coating, one by one into hot oil and cook until crispy and golden brown, approximately 8 minutes per batch, flipping once. Repeat with the remaining chicken wings.

5. Meanwhile, stir together honey, Sriracha, ketchup, and lemon juice.

6. Toss fried chicken wings into the sauce and gently toss to coat.

7. Serve with a garnish of toasted sesame seeds.

Thai-Style Chicken Wings

Here is another Asian inspired chicken wing recipe. This time, Thai cuisine is lending its amazing mix of sweet and sticky and savory. The flavors simply meld well and explode like a bomb as you pop the wings onto the grill. What you get is a delicious finger food idea, which you can serve with a simple dipping sauce or a veggie side dish to make a good meal for lunch or dinner.

Servings: 4

Cook time: 30 minutes

Ingredients:

- 2 lb. Chicken Wings, Separated
- 1 Lime, Sliced into Wedges
- 1 tsp. Ground Black Pepper
- 2 tbsp. Cilantro Stems, Finely Chopped
- 5 Garlic Cloves, Minced
- 5 tbsp. Fish Sauce
- 4 tbsp. Thai Sweet Chili Sauce

Instructions:

1. Add the chicken wings in a bowl and rub with minced garlic and cilantro stems.

2. Pour sweet chili sauce and fish sauce, then, sprinkle with freshly ground black pepper. Mix to blend and set aside for at least an hour or overnight to marinade.

3. When the chicken wings are ready, preheat the grill on high and cook the chicken wings for about 8 minutes per batch, flipping to get an evenly charred and cooked meat.

4. Serve with lime wedges on the side.

Tandoori Chicken Wings

There are so many things to flavor up chicken wings. Indian spices and seasonings will be a good candidate if you want to go to the other way of the classic buffalo. These Tandoori Chicken Wings, for one, feature a unique blend of bold flavors, which will give your dinner a different treatment, from the taste to the aroma. It's a certified crowd-pleaser, especially when served with suitable sauces, just like the tangy blue cheese dressing or some spiced yogurt.

Servings: 6

Cook time: 1 hour 30 minutes

Ingredients:

- 2 lb. Chicken Wings, Separated and Pat Dried
- 1 tbsp. Dried Fenugreek Leaves
- 1 tbsp. Ginger, Peeled
- 8 Cloves Garlic, Peeled
- 2 tbsp. Cilantro, Chopped
- ¾ c. Plain Yogurt
- 2 tbsp. Lemon Juice
- 1 tbsp. Water
- 2 tsp. Gram Masala
- ½ tsp. Turmeric Powder
- 2 tsp. Red Chili Powder
- 2 tsp. Kosher Salt

Instructions:

1. Using a traditional mortar and pestle, make a paste from the combination of ginger, garlic, and 1 tablespoon of water. If you don't have mortar and pestle at home, you can always use a food processor.

2. Transfer the paste to a large bowl. Then, add yogurt, garam masala, fenugreek leaves, lemon juice, turmeric powder, chili powder, and salt. Mix to blend.

3. Add chicken wings and toss, making sure the meats are evenly coated with the marinade.

4. Wrap the bowl with a sheet of cling wrap and set aside in the fridge to chill for an hour or so.

5. When the chicken wings are almost ready, preheat the oven to 400 degrees F.

6. Place the wire rack on top of a baking tray and arrange the chicken wings on top of the rack.

7. Bake for 20 minutes or more until cooked through.

8. Place chicken wings in a serving platter, garnish with freshly chopped cilantro, and serve.

Brazilian Style Fried Chicken Wings

Asian flavors aside, there's this recipe that would allow you to a different take on chicken wings, although it is not too far from the classic Buffalo recipe. By doing a Brazilian treatment to your meat, you can say goodbye to boredom and embrace the excitement. This recipe presents some crispy, well-seasoned, and fabulously crunchy chicken wings, which you will love sharing with your loved ones on a game day or serve it with rice and beans to turn it into a wholesome family meal.

Servings: 6

Cook time: 50 minutes

Ingredients:

- 2 lb. Chicken Wings, Separated
- 1 Lime, Sliced into Wedges
- Juice Of 3 Limes
- 5 Cloves Garlic, Sliced
- 5 Cloves Garlic, Minced
- 1 tbsp. Parsley, Chopped
- ¼ c. Olive Oil
- 3 c. Vegetable Oil
- ½ c. All-Purpose Flour
- Pinch of Red Pepper Flakes
- Salt and Pepper to Taste

Instructions:

1. Whisk together lime juice and minced garlic in a large bowl.

2. Sprinkle salt and pepper and toss chicken to coat evenly. Cover with a sheet of plastic wrap. Then, set aside in the fridge to marinade for an hour or overnight.

3. Next, take the wings out of the marinade and pat dry with paper towels.

4. Sprinkle flour and toss to coat.

5. Heat oil in the pan and fry the chicken wings for about 6 minutes per batch, flipping once, until crispy and golden brown.

6. Transfer fried chicken wings to a paper towel lined plate to remove excess oil, then, place in a serving platter.

7. Then, use the same pan, fry the sliced garlic and scatter over chicken wings.

8. Garnish it with fresh chopped parsley, a pinch of red pepper flakes, and some lime wedges on the side.

Chicken Wings and Noodles Stir Fry

Who says chicken wings shall only be eaten by the fingers? With this recipe, where you add noodles and veggies into the mix, you can elevate chicken wings to a midweek meal that's so satisfying and so filling! You can choose different veggie mixes for this stir-fry recipe, whatever is in season and whatever your family likes.

Servings: 4

Cook time: 45 minutes

Ingredients:

- 2 lb. Chicken Wings, Separated
- 1 lb. Hokkien Noodles, Blanched
- 1 Bunch Bok Choy, Chopped
- 1 Carrot, Shredded
- 1 Red Capsicum, Seeded and Sliced
- 2 Spring Onions, Sliced Into 1-Inch Pieces
- 1 tbsp. Ginger, Grated
- 2 Cloves Garlic, Sliced
- 1 tbsp. Toasted Sesame Seeds
- 1/3 c. Kecap Manis
- 1 tbsp. Oyster Sauce
- 2 tbsp. Vegetable Oil
- 2 tsp. Sesame Oil

Instructions:

1. Heat oil in a wok on medium-high and brown chicken pieces for about 10 minutes per batch.

2. Put back all the chicken into the wok and stir in carrots, capsicum, ginger, and garlic.

3. Add bok choy and green onions and cook for about 1 minute more.

4. In a small bowl, stir together kecap manis, oyster sauce, and sesame oil.

5. Pour mixture into the pan and toss noodles. Cook for about 2 minutes.

6. Serve with a sprinkle of toasted sesame seeds on top.

Chicken Wings Sour Soup

Soups are comforting. They remind you of a tight, warm hug. And every time they appear at the dining table, they light up everyone's faces. Who says you can only serve chicken wings dry or saucy? You can add them to soups and level up their appeal even more. If you are only after the soup, this is where the chicken wings could go. But of course, you would want some meat, too, so add up all the cut-up pieces. You may even put chicken backs and necks and other meaty chicken parts as well.

Servings: 8

Cook time: 55 minutes

Ingredients:

- 3 lb. Chicken Wings, Separated
- Juice Of 3 Pcs Lemons
- 2 Potatoes, Peeled and Diced
- 2 Carrots, Grated
- ¼ c. Parsnip, Grated
- 2 Zucchini, Diced
- 2 tbsp. Celery, Grated
- 1 Red Bell Pepper, Diced
- ½ c. Cilantro, Chopped
- 1 Onion, Diced
- 3 Eggs
- 1 (14 oz.) Can Diced Tomatoes
- Salt and Pepper to Taste

Instructions:

1. Place chicken wings in a stockpot and cover with enough water.

2. Boil for about 20 minutes on medium fire.

3. Add potatoes and let it simmer for another 10 minutes, until the potatoes are tender.

4. Add the remaining ingredients, except for eggs, diced tomatoes and fresh lemon juice. Let it cook for another 20 minutes.

5. Finally, stir in tomatoes and lemon juice.

6. Beat in the eggs into the soup, adjust seasoning, and serve hot.

Rotisserie Chicken Wings

The rotisserie is a great spot for some delicious chicken wing treats. If you do not fancy a whole bird and you simply crave for wings, you can simply pop them into the rotisserie basket, secure the lid, and let it cook nicely in a slow cook manner. But of course, the key to tasty chicken wings is your seasoning. So here, we have the recipe for you.

Servings: 6

Cook time: 1 hour 25 minutes

Ingredients:

- 4 lb. Chicken Wings, Separated into Wingettes And Drumettes
- ½ tbsp. Ancho Chili Pepper
- ¼ tsp. Dried Ground Thyme
- ½ tbsp. Smoked Paprika
- ½ tsp. Dried Mustard Powder
- ¾ tsp. Paprika
- ¼ tsp. Dried Oregano
- ½ tbsp. Onion Powder
- ½ tsp. Garlic Powder
- ¾ tsp. Cumin
- ¾ tsp. Chili Powder
- ¾ tbsp. Brown Sugar
- ½ tbsp. Kosher Salt
- ¼ tsp. Black Pepper
- ½ tsp. Cayenne Pepper
- 2 tbsp. Vegetable Oil

Instructions:

1. Mix the ingredients except for chicken wings and oil, until well blended.

2. Transfer wings to a resealable plastic bag and pour in oil.

3. Add half of the dry rub and massage onto chicken wings. Seal and set aside in the fridge to chill for about an hour.

4. When the wings are almost ready, fire up the grill to medium high.

5. Place wings onto a rotisserie attachment with a pan underneath, close the lid, and let it cook for about 20-30 minutes.

6. Put the wings to a serving platter and serve with our favorite sauce.

Bacon-Wrapped Chicken Wings

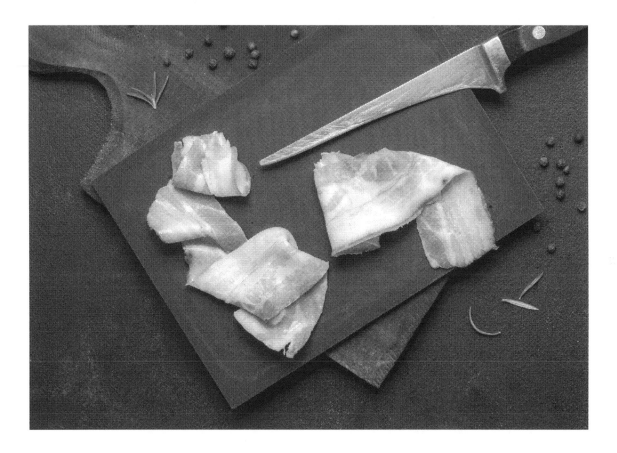

What's better than chicken wings? Well, chicken wings wrapped in bacon strips will do, don't you think so? Imagine the tasty and flavorful meat is wrapped in a slice of bacon? Yummy, right? That's exactly what this dish is. It's yummy and will surely make your parties eventful if you add a platter of this in the buffet spread.

Servings: 16

Cook time: 1 hour 55 minutes

Ingredients:

- 4 lb. chicken wings, split at the joints
- 1 lb. bacon, halved crosswise
- ½ c. BBQ sauce, divided
- 1 tbsp. Worcestershire sauce
- ¼ c. fresh lime juice
- 1 tsp. cayenne pepper
- Cooking spray

Instructions:

1. Whisk together Worcestershire sauce, lime juice and cayenne pepper in a large bowl.

2. Coat the chicken wings evenly. Set it with a plastic wrap set aside in the fridge for about an hour.

3. When the wings are almost ready, preheat the oven to 400 degrees F. Arrange a wire rack on top of a baking sheet. Then, lightly grease with some cooking spray.

4. Lift the chicken wings from the marinade, discarding the liquid, and wrap each piece with a slice of bacon. Then, secure the ends with a toothpick.

5. Arrange bacon wrapped wings onto the prepared rack, brush generously with BBQ sauce, and bake for about 30 minutes. Flip halfway through and brush again with the remaining BBQ sauce.

6. Serve and enjoy.

Glazed Mongolian Chicken Wings

With the help of this recipe, I guarantee you will never want to order Chinese takeout ever again. Sweet and spicy in flavor, this is a wing recipe I know you will want to make over and over again.

Servings: 1

Cook time: 1 hour 20 minutes

Ingredients:

- 1 ½ lb. Chicken Wings
- 2 tbsp. Vegetable Oil
- Salt and Black Pepper
- ¼ c. Soy Sauce, Low Sodium
- ¼ c. Honey
- 2 tbsp. rice Wine Vinegar
- 1 tbsp. Sriracha Sauce
- 3 cloves minced Garlic
- 1 tbsp. Ginger, grated
- Green Onions, Thinly Sliced and For Garnish
- Sesame Seeds for Garnish

Instructions:

1. Preheat the oven to 425 degrees. Set the wire rack on top of a baking sheet.

2. Put the chicken wings and vegetable oil in a dish. Top with a tablespoon of salt and black pepper. Move to the wire rack.

3. Put it into the oven to bake for 45 to 50 minutes or until crispy.

4. Set a pan in a medium to high heat, add in the soy sauce, vinegar, honey, Sriracha sauce, minced garlic and grated ginger. Stir well to mix. Allow to come to a simmer. Cook for 10 minutes or until reduced.

5. Transfer the wings into a bowl. Pour the glaze over the top. Toss well to mix. Put the wings back onto the wire rack.

6. Place back into the oven to broil for 2 to 3 minutes.

7. Remove. Lastly, serve immediately with a garnish of sliced green onions and sesame seeds.

BBQ Root Beer Wings

This is the only barbecue wing recipe you will need this summer season. These wings are great to make for your next family barbecue or whenever you are craving barbecue chicken wings.

Servings: 6 to 8

Cook time: 15 minutes

Ingredients:

- ¾ c. Root Beer
- 1 c. Ketchup
- 1 tbsp. Sugar, Light Brown
- 2 tbsp. Honey
- 1 tbsp. Worcestershire Sauce
- 1 lime Juiced
- ½ tsp. Garlic, Powdered
- ½ tsp. Onion, Powdered

For the Wings:

- 3 lb. Chicken Wings
- 2 tbsp. vegetable Oil
- Dash of Salt and Black Pepper

Instructions:

1. Prepare for the sauce. Add the root beer, ketchup, light brown sugar, tea, lime juice, garlic powder, onion powder and Worcestershire sauce in a pan over low to medium heat. Now, whisk to blend. Cook for 8 to 10 minutes or until softened.

2. Preheat your oven to 425 degrees F. Then, put the baking sheet on your wire rack.

3. Prepare the wings. In a bowl, add in the chicken wings and vegetable oil. Toss well to coat. Then, sprinkle a dash of salt and black pepper.

4. Put the chicken wings onto a wire rack. Set in the oven for 55 to 1 hour.

5. Brush the sauce over the wings. Place into your oven to broil for 4 minutes or until caramelized. Remove and serve.

Miso Chicken Wings

These are the perfect wings to make whenever you are craving something with an authentic Asian flavor. One taste, and I know you will totally love it!

Servings: 6

Cook time: 1 hour

Ingredients:

- 12 Chicken Wings
- 2 tbsp. Canola Oil
- A dash Salt and Black Pepper
- 1 c. Shiro Miso
- 2 tbsp. Lime Juice
- 1 tsp. Ginger, Grated
- 1 tsp. Asian Fish Sauce
- 1 Thai Bird Chile
- 3 tbsp. Sugar, Turbinado
- Cilantro Leaves, For Garnish
- Lime Wedges, For Garnish

Instructions:

1. Preheat the oven to 400 degrees F.

2. In a bowl, add in the chicken wings and canola oil. Sprinkle it with salt and black pepper. Toss well to coat. Transfer onto a baking sheet.

3. Next, set in the oven for 40 minutes or until crispy.

4. Set a pan over a medium heat, add in the shiro miso, lime juice, grated ginger, Asian fish sauce, bird chile and turbinado sugar. Whisk well to mix. Add in 3 tablespoons of water. Cook over low heat approximately for 3 to 5 minutes or until thick in consistency. Remove from heat.

5. Brush the wings with the glaze. Put it back in your oven for 10 minutes or until golden.

6. Then, transfer the chicken wings onto a serving plate.

7. Serve with a garnish of chopped cilantro leaves and lime wedges.

Jack Daniel's Chicken Wings

These delicious chicken wings are absolutely fabulous. They're definitely a must make during your next cookout.

Servings: 60

Cook time: 30 minutes

Ingredients:

- 30 Chicken Wings, Halved at Their Joints
- 1 red Chili, Chopped
- Honey
- 6 tbsp. Soy Sauce
- ½ inch Ginger, Grated
- 7 Thyme Leaves, Chopped
- 4 tbsp. Jack Daniels
- 2 tsp. Cumin, Powdered
- 2 tbsp. Light Brown Sugar
- 2 tbsp. Extra Virgin Olive Oil

Instructions:

1. In a Ziploc bag, add in all of the ingredients except for the chicken wing halves. Stir well to mix.

2. Add in the chicken wings and seal the bag. Toss the wings to coat.

3. Next, place into the fridge to marinate overnight.

4. Preheat an oven to 425 degrees.

5. Then, place the chicken wings onto a baking sheet. Set in the oven for 25 to 30 minutes or until golden.

6. Remove and serve immediately.

Chicken Parm Wings

This is a delicious chicken wing dish you can make whenever you are craving authentic Italian cuisine.

Servings: 4

Cook time: 50 minutes

Ingredients:

- 1 lb. Chicken Wings
- 23 oz. Ragu Sauce, Evenly Divided
- ¾ c. Italian Breadcrumbs
- ¼ c. grated Parmesan Cheese, Extra for Garnish
- Salt and Black Pepper (Dash)
- Parsley, Chopped and For Serving

Instructions:

1. Preheat the oven to 425 degrees. Put the wire rack in the baking sheet.

2. In a bowl, add in the 1 ½ cups of Ragu sauce. In a separate bowl, add in the Italian breadcrumbs, grated Parmesan cheese, dash of salt and black pepper. Stir well to mix.

3. Dip the chicken wings into the Ragu sauce. Toss into the breadcrumb mix until coated.

4. Transfer the wings onto the wire rack.

5. Put it inside the oven to bake for 30 to 35 minutes or until crispy.

6. Remove and serve with a garnish with Parmesan cheese and chopped parsley.

Bloody Mary Chicken Wings

There is no secret that booze and wings go hand and hand excellently. This is a dish that pairs both of these excellently to make a filling meal you won't be able to get enough of.

Servings: 8 to 10

Cook time: 2 hours

Ingredients:

For the Wings:

- 3 lb. Chicken Wings
- 1 tbsp. Vegetable Oil
- Dash of Celery Salt
- Dash of Black Pepper
- 3 c. Tomato Juice
- 2/3 c. Vodka
- ¾ c. Sugar, Light Brown
- 1/3 c. Hot Sauce
- 1 tbsp. Horseradish
- 1 tbsp. Worcestershire Sauce
- 1 Lemon, Juice Only
- Dash of Salt and Black Pepper

For the Dip:

- 2/3 c. Sour Cream
- 2 tsp. Horseradish
- 2 tsp. Dill

Instructions:

1. Preheat the oven to 425 degrees F.

2. In a bowl, add in the chicken wings. Drizzle the olive oil over the wings. Season the wings with the celery salt and dash of black pepper.

3. In a separate bowl, add in the tomato juice, vodka, light brown sugar, hot sauce, fresh lemon juice, Worcestershire sauce and horseradish. Whisk well to mix. Give it a taste by adding a salt and black pepper.

4. Pour over the top of the wings. Cover with a sheet of plastic wrap. Set into the fridge to marinate for 1 hour.

5. Transfer the wings onto a baking sheet. Put it inside the oven for 45 minutes or until crispy. Remove and set aside to cool slightly.

6. Heat a pan in a medium heat then add in the marinade. Allow to come to a simmer. Cook approximately for 5 to 10 minutes or until reduced.

7. Brush the wings with the sauce. Then, place back into the oven to broil for 3 minutes.

8. Prepare the dip. In a bowl, add in the sour cream, horseradish and chopped dill.

9. Serve the chicken wings immediately with the dip.

Buffalo Shuffle Chicken Wings

Buffalo Chicken Wings are the staple among just about any hungry man out there; the spicy pepper sauce is so popular that it is also used to other special dish as well.

Servings: 4

Cook time: 1 hour

Ingredients:

- 2 ½ lb. chicken wings
- ¼ c. hot sauce
- 1 stick melted butter
- Celery and carrot sticks
- Bleu cheese dip

Instructions:

1. Preheat oven to 400 degrees F.

2. Mix hot sauce and butter in a saucepan on stove. Let simmer on low for 5-7 minutes.

3. Using tongs, dip wings in hot sauce /butter mix.

4. Place dipped wings in a roasting pan and place in preheated oven.

5. Bake for about an hour turning once at the hallway point.

6. Remove from oven. Let sit in pan a few minutes and then use tongs to move wings from the roasting pan to serving platter.

7. Serve the wings with the celery and carrot sticks and bleu cheese dip.

8. I like to add additional crumbled blue cheese to the bleu cheese dip.

Honey Barbecue Chicken Wings

This is a sweet tasting chicken wing that every picky eater is going to fall in love with. It is sweet in flavor; it will satisfy any strong sweet tooth.

Servings: 6

Cook time: 1 hour 15 minutes

Ingredients:

- 2 lb. Chicken Wings
- 2 tbsp. Extra Virgin Olive Oil
- 1 tbsp. smoked Paprika
- 1 tbsp. powdered Garlic
- Salt and Black Pepper (Dash)
- 4 tbsp. Butter
- 1 c. Barbecue Sauce
- ¼ c. Honey
- 2 tsp. Hot Sauce
- Ranch Dressing, For Dipping

Instructions:

1. Preheat oven then place a wire rack over baking sheet.

2. In a bowl, add in the chicken wings and the olive oil. Season with the smoked paprika, powdered garlic, black pepper and dash of salt. Toss well to mix. Transfer onto the wire rack.

3. Set in the oven for 55 minutes to 1 hour or until crispy.

4. Prepare the sauce. Heat up the pan in a low heat in the butter. Add in the honey, barbecue sauce, and hot sauce. Whisk to mix and allow to come to a simmer. Cook for 5 minutes or until thick in consistency. Remove from heat.

5. Preheat the oven to broil.

6. Transfer the wings into a bowl. Add in the sauce. Toss well to coat. Transfer onto a wire rack. Set in the oven for 3 minutes or until caramelized.

7. Serve immediately with the ranch dressing.

Crispy Chicken Wings

There is no other chicken wing recipe that is as easy to prepare and fun to eat as this chicken wing dish.

Servings: 40

Cook time: 1 hour 25 minutes

Ingredients:

- 40 Chicken Wings
- 2 tsp. Salt
- 1 tsp. Black Pepper
- 2 tbsp. powdered Garlic, Extra for Dusting
- 2 tbsp. Salt, Seasoned
- 1/3 c. extra virgin olive Oil, As Needed
- 1 c. grated Parmesan Cheese, Evenly Divided
- 2 c. All-Purpose Flour
- 3 c. Peanut Oil

Instructions:

1. Preheat the oven to 375 degrees F.

2. In a bowl, add in the olive oil, seasoned salt, powdered garlic and ½ cup of grated parmesan cheese.

3. Give it a taste by adding a salt and black pepper. Add in the chicken wings. Toss well until coated.

4. Transfer the chicken wings onto a baking sheet.

5. Set in the oven for 1 hour or until cooked through. Remove and transfer into a bowl. Add in the all-purpose flour and toss to coat. Place back onto the baking sheet.

6. In your pot set over medium to high heat, add in the peanut oil. Heat up the oil until 350 degrees. Add in the chicken wings. Fry for 1 minute or until crispy.

7. Place a plate with paper towels to drain. Serve with a garnish of grated parmesan cheese.

Shanghai Chicken Wings

These tasty chicken wings baked in a sweet marinade sauce may be served in the sauce or drained and reheated for easier eating.

Servings: 8

Cook time: 1 hour 50 minutes

Ingredients:

- 2½ lb. chicken wings
- 2 c. chicken broth
- 1 c. brown sugar
- ¼ c. granulated sugar
- 1 tbsp. fresh grated gingerroot
- ¼ c. 7UP
- ¼ c. soy sauce

Instructions:

1. Preheat oven to 400° F.

2. Rinse and pat the chicken dry.

3. In a bowl, add together the broth, sugars, ginger, wine, and soy sauce.

4. Place the chicken wings in 9" × 11" pan or casserole. Pour on the marinade. Let set for 1 hour and bake for 45 minutes.

5. Serve immediately, or remove from the sauce, reserving it, and store overnight to reheat the next day. Brush lightly with the sauce before heating.

Roasted Chicken Wings with Sumac, Lemon & Garlic

With an irresistible balance of spice, sweetness, and salt, and seared crispy skin, these chicken wings make a very enticing snack.

Servings: 4

Cook time: 50 minutes

Ingredients:

- 2 tbsp. Olive Oil
- 1 tbsp. Honey
- 2 Garlic Cloves, Crushed
- 1 tbsp. Sumac
- 2 tsp. Sea Salt Flakes, Crushed
- Grated Zest Of 1 Unwaxed Lemon, + 1 Lemon, Cut into Wedges, To Serve
- 1 lb. Chicken Wings, Cut into Drumettes And Wingettes
- ¼ c. Greek-Style Plain Yogurt, To Serve

Instructions:

1. Preheat the oven to 425°F. Mix together the oil, honey, garlic, sumac, salt, and lemon zest in a large roasting pan. Add the chicken & mix till well coated.

2. Roast the chicken at the top of the oven for 25 minutes, or until cooked through and slightly charred with a crispy skin, shaking the pan halfway through cooking to turn the pieces.

3. Let the chicken rest for 5 minutes. Then, serve with the Greek yogurt and lemon wedges for squeezing over the chicken.

Hot Chicken Wings

Crisp skin, tender meat, and finger-licking sauce. You're all ready to enjoy the comfort of your home.

Servings: 2

Cook time: 35 minutes

Ingredients:

For the Blue Cheese Dressing

- ½ c. Blue Cheese
- ⅓ c. Buttermilk
- ¼ c. Sour Cream
- 3 tbsp. Mayonnaise
- 2 tbsp. Apple Cider Vinegar

For the Sauce

- 1 c. (2 Sticks) Salted Butter
- 2 (5 oz.) Bottles Hot Sauce

For the Wings

- Peanut Oil or Coconut Oil, For Frying
- 1 c. All-Purpose Flour
- 1 c. Breadcrumbs
- 1 tbsp. Garlic Powder
- 1 tbsp. Sea Salt
- 1 tbsp. Red Pepper Flakes
- 2 Eggs
- 2 tbsp. Apple Cider Vinegar
- 12 Chicken Pieces, Wings and Drumsticks, Patted Dry
- Celery Sticks, For Serving

Instructions:

To Make the Blue Cheese Dressing

1. Combine all together the blue cheese, buttermilk, sour cream, mayonnaise, and apple cider vinegar. Cover and refrigerate until needed.

To Make the Sauce

2. In a saucepan on med-low heat, melt butter. Whisk in the hot sauce. Reduce & simmer the sauce while you cook the wings, stirring occasionally.

To Make the Wings

3. In the skillet over high heat, heat 1 inch of peanut oil to 375°F.

4. On a clean work surface, line up 2 small bowls. In the first bowl, mix the flour, breadcrumbs, garlic powder, sea salt, and red pepper flakes. In the second bowl, whisk eggs & apple cider vinegar.

5. Working 1 piece at a time, put the chicken into the egg mixture and then into the flour mixture. Add to the hot oil and fry approximately for 2 to 3 minutes per side.

6. Dunk the cooked chicken in the hot sauce and transfer to a wire rack to cool. Serve.

Japanese Chicken Wings

Integrate Japanese cuisine into classic American with this delicious recipe.

Servings: 4

Cook time: 55 minutes

Ingredients:

- 3 lb. Chicken wings, separated at joints, tips discarded
- 1 Egg, lightly beaten
- 1 c. all-purpose Flour, for coating
- 1 c. Butter

Sauce:

- 3 tbsp. Soy sauce
- 3 tbsp. Water
- 1 c. white Sugar
- ½ c. white Vinegar
- ½ tsp. Garlic powder
- 1 tsp. Salt

Instructions:

1. Preheat oven and dip wings into egg then lightly coat using flour.

2. Heat the butter into a skillet over high heat.

3. Fry chicken wings until brown then place into a roasting pan.

4. Combine the vinegar, soy sauce, garlic powder, water, sugar, and salt into a bowl. Pour over chicken wings.

5. Bake into oven for 45 minutes, basting wings often with sauce.

Smokestack Chicken Wings

These wings are smothered in a spiced butter sauce that makes these wings even more delicious.

Servings: 6

Cook time: 4 hours 25 minutes

Ingredients:

- 1 tbsp. Salt
- 2¼ tsp. Sweet paprika
- 1 ½ tsp. Garlic, powdered
- 1 ½ tsp. Onion, powdered
- 1 ½ tsp. Thyme
- 1 ½ tsp. Oregano
- ¾ tsp. Black pepper
- ¾ tsp. White pepper
- ½ tsp. Sage, dried
- ½ tsp. Cayenne pepper
- 2 ½ lb. Chicken wings
- 16 tbsp. melted Butter
- ½ c. Hot sauce
- ¼ c. Old Bay seasoning
- 1 Lemon, juice only

Instructions:

1. In a bowl, add in the salt, sweet paprika, powdered garlic, powder onion, dried thyme, dried oregano, dried sage, cayenne pepper, black and white pepper. Stir well to mix. Add in the chicken wings. Toss well to coat.

2. Cover & put into the fridge for 4 hours.

3. Prepare the sauce. In a bowl, add in the butter, hot sauce, Old Bay seasoning and lemon juice. Stir well to mix. Pour half of this mix into a separate bowl. Set aside.

4. Preheat an outdoor grill to 225 degrees.

5. Add the chicken wings into the sauce. Toss to coat. Place onto the grill. Cook for 25 minutes, flipping once through the cooking process.

6. Transfer back into the sauce. Toss again to coat. Serve immediately.

Garlic and Ranch Chicken Wings

These wings are incredibly juicy, crispy, and made with a ranch flavor that everybody will love.

Servings: 6

Cook time: 3 hours 45 minutes

Ingredients:

- 5 lb. Chicken Wings
- 2 tsp. Paprika, Smoked
- 2 tbsp. Ranch Dressing, Dried
- 1 tbsp. Salt
- 2 tsp. Powdered Garlic
- 3 tbsp. Mayonnaise

Instructions:

1. In a bowl, add in the chicken wings, smoked paprika, dried ranch dressing, dash of salt, powdered garlic and mayonnaise. Toss well to coat. Cover & set into the fridge for 3 hours.

2. Add the parchment paper in the baking sheet. Put the chicken wings onto the baking pan.

3. Put it inside the oven for 45 minutes at 400 degrees or until golden.

4. Flip and continue to bake approximately for 10 minutes or until crispy on the bottom of the wings.

5. Remove and serve immediately.

Cajun Spiced Chicken Wings

These delicious chicken wings contain a touch of honey and spice.

Servings: 10

Cook time: 40 minutes

Ingredients:

- 3 lb. Chicken Wings
- 1/3 c. Cajun Seasoning
- 1 c. Barbecue Sauce
- 2 tbsp. Honey
- 1 tbsp. Sriracha Sauce
- 1 Lime, Juice and Zest Only)

Instructions:

1. Preheat the oven to 350 degrees. Grease two baking sheets.

2. Place the chicken wings onto the baking sheets. Season with the Cajun seasoning

3. Set in the oven for 30 minutes.

4. Prepare the sauce. In a bowl, add in the barbecue sauce, honey, Sriracha sauce, lime juice and lime zest. Stir well until mixed.

5. Remove the chicken wings and baste with the sauce. Set it back in the oven for an additional 10 minutes or until the sauce on the wings are caramelized.

6. Remove and rest approximately for 5 minutes before serving.

Vietnamese Chicken Wings

These are the perfect chicken wings for you to make whenever you want to try something new. They are packed with a unique exotic flavor I know you will find interesting.

Servings: 8

Cook time: 35 minutes

Ingredients:

- 1 ¼ lb. Chicken Wings
- 2 tbsp. Sweet Soy Sauce
- 1 tbsp. Chili Paste
- 1 tbsp. Worcestershire Sauce
- Cilantro, Chopped and For Garnish

Instructions:

1. Preheat the oven to 475 degrees. Add a sheet of aluminum foil onto a baking sheet.

2. Pat dry the chicken wings with a few paper towels. Place onto the baking sheet.

3. Next, drizzle 1 to 2 tablespoons of olive oil over the wings. Give it a taste by adding a dash of salt and black pepper. Mix well to coat.

4. Set in the oven approximately for 20 to 25 minutes or until cooked through.

5. Prepare the sauce. In a bowl, add in the sweet soy sauce, Worcestershire sauce and chili sauce. Whisk until mixed. Add in the chicken wings, then toss to coat. Place the chicken wings back onto a baking sheet.

6. Place into the oven to roast for 6 to 8 minutes or until browned.

7. Remove and top off with extra sauce.

8. Lastly, serve with a garnish of the chopped cilantro.

Smoking Sweet Chicken Wings

This is a delicious chicken wing dish everybody won't be able to resist. Made with a sweet cherry barbecue glaze, I know this is a chicken dish you will want to make as often as possible.

Servings: 4

Cook time: 40 minutes

Ingredients:

- 2 tbsp. butter
- ½ sweet onion, thinly sliced
- 1 habanero chile, thinly sliced
- ¾ c. cherry preserves
- ½ c. lime juice
- Dash salt and black pepper
- 3 ½ lb. chicken wings

Instructions:

1. Heat a pan in a medium heat firstly and add in the butter. Once melted, add in the sliced sweet onion. Cook for 5 minutes or until soft.

2. Add in ¾ of the sliced chile. Continue to cook for 1 minute.

3. Transfer into a blender with the lime juice. Puree on the highest setting until smooth in consistency. Pour into a saucepan set over high heat. Allow to come to a boil. Give it a taste by adding a salt and black pepper. Transfer into a bowl.

4. Preheat the oven to broil.

5. Season the chicken wings with a dash of salt and black pepper. Place onto the grill. Grill for 20 minutes or until crispy. Transfer into a bowl.

6. Add 1/3 of the glaze over the wings. Toss well to mix. Place back onto the grill. Cook for 2 minutes or until caramelized. Transfer back into the bowl. Then, pour 1/3 of the glaze over the wings. Toss again.

7. Serve the wings with the remaining glaze.

Ginger and Honey Hot Wings Chicken Wings

These traditional hot wings are perfect for making whenever you need to make dinner for a large group of people.

Servings: 2 to 4

Cook time: 1 hour

Ingredients:

- 2 tbsp. all-purpose flour
- 1 tsp. salt
- 1 tsp. powdered Sichuan peppercorns
- ¼ tsp. powdered five spice
- 2 lb. chicken wingettes and drumettes
- 2 ½ tbsp. hot sauce
- 2 tbsp. butter
- ½ tbsp. soy sauce
- 2 tbsp. honey
- 2 tbsp. ginger, minced
- 2 tbsp. scallions

Instructions:

1. Preheat the oven to 500 degrees. Wrap the baking sheet with an aluminum foil. Grease with cooking spray.

2. In a bowl, add in the all-purpose flour, dash of salt, peppercorns and powdered five spices. Stir well to mix. Add in the chicken wingettes and drumettes. Toss to coat.

3. Transfer the chicken onto the baking sheet. Grease the chicken with cooking spray.

4. Put in inside the oven to bake for 45 minutes or until crispy.

5. In a bowl, add in the soy sauce, butter, minced ginger and scallions. Stir well to mix. Add in the roasted chicken and toss to coat.

6. Serve with a topping of scallions.

Maple Chipotle Hot Wings Chicken Wings

This is the perfect wing recipe whenever you want to challenge yourself with a bit of heat. Be sure to drink milk with these wings.

Servings: 2 to 4

Cook time: 1 hour

Ingredients:

- 2 tbsp. All-Purpose Flour
- 1 tsp. Salt
- 1 tsp. Dried Sage
- 2 lb. Chicken Wingettes And Drumettes
- 2 tbsp. Butter, Melted
- 1 (14.5 oz.) Can Chipotle Peppers, Sliced
- 2 tbsp. Maple Syrup

Instructions:

1. Preheat the oven to 500 degrees F firstly. Place a sheet of aluminum foil onto the baking sheet. Grease with cooking spray.

2. In a bowl, add the all-purpose flour, dash of salt and dried sage. Stir well to mix. Then, add in the chicken and toss well to coat.

3. Transfer the chicken onto a baking sheet. Grease the chicken with cooking spray.

4. Put in inside the oven for 45 minutes or until crispy.

5. In a bowl, add in the hot sauce, melted butter, sliced chipotle peppers and maple syrup. Stir well to mix. Add in the roasted chicken and toss to coat.

6. Serve immediately.

Spiced Apricot Chicken Wings

While apricots and chicken wings may seem like an unappealing combination, you will think differently once you try these wings for yourself.

Servings: 6

Cook time: 40 minutes

Ingredients:

- ½ c. Apricot Wood Chips
- ½ c. Apricot Preserves
- 2 tbsp. Worcestershire Sauce
- 2 tbsp. Light Brown Sugar
- 1 tbsp. Soy Sauce
- 1 tbsp. Dijon Mustard
- 1 tbsp. Salt
- 2 tsp. Black Pepper
- 1 tsp. Powdered Garlic
- 1 tsp. Sweet Paprika
- ½ tsp. Cayenne Pepper
- ¼ tsp. Powdered Ginger
- 3 lb. Chicken Wings

Instructions:

1. First, preheat an outdoor grill to medium or high heat. Wrap the apricot wood chips in aluminum foil. Pierce with a skewer and place into the grill. Cover and cook for 5 minutes or until the wood chips begin to smoke.

2. In a bowl, add in the preserves, Worcestershire sauce, light brown sugar, soy sauce, Dijon mustard, powdered garlic, sweet paprika, cayenne pepper and powdered ginger. Then, add salt and black pepper and stir well to mix.

3. Pour half of the sauce into a separate bowl. In the separate bowl, add in the chicken wings. Toss well to coat. Set aside to rest for 5 minutes.

4. Place the chicken wings onto the grill. Cover and cook approximately for 20 to 25 minutes or until cooked through.

5. Remove and rest for 5 minutes.

6. Serve with the remaining sauce.

Mango Curry Hot Wings

These wings, while spicy, contain a hint of sweetness that makes them irresistible. Serve these to add a sweet flair to your next wing night.

Servings: 2 to 4

Cook time: 1 hour

Ingredients:

- 2 lb. Chicken Wingettes And Drumettes
- 1 tsp. Salt
- 2 tbsp. All-Purpose Flour
- 2 tsp. Powdered Curry
- 2 ½ tbsp. Hot Sauce
- 2 tbsp. Butter
- 2 tbsp. Major Grey Chutney
- Pistachios, Chopped

Instructions:

1. First, preheat the oven to 500 degrees. Place a sheet of aluminum foil onto your baking sheet. Grease with cooking spray.

2. Next, in a bowl, add in the all-purpose flour, dash of salt and powdered curry. Add in the chicken wingettes and drumettes. Toss well until coated.

3. Transfer onto the baking sheet and grease the chicken with cooking spray.

4. Place into the oven to roast for 45 minutes or until crispy. Remove and set aside to cool.

5. In a bowl, add in the hot sauce, butter and major grey chutney. Whisk well until mixed. Add in the chicken wings, then toss well until coated.

6. Serve with a topping of chopped pistachios.

Garlic and Ranch Chicken Wings

This is a great chicken wing recipe you can make in a hurry. These wings are incredibly juicy, crispy and made with a ranch flavor everybody will love.

Servings: 6

Cook time: 4 hours and 15 minutes

Ingredients:

- 5 lb. chicken wings
- 2 tsp. smoked paprika
- 2 tbsp. dried ranch dressing
- 1 tbsp. salt
- 2 tsp. powdered garlic
- 3 tbsp. mayonnaise

Instructions:

1. In a bowl, add in the chicken wings, smoked paprika, dried ranch dressing, dash of salt, powdered garlic and mayonnaise. Toss well to coat. Cover and set into your fridge to chill for 3 hours.

2. Place a sheet of parchment paper onto a baking sheet. Then, place the chicken wings onto the baking sheet.

3. Put it inside the oven for 45 minutes at 400 degrees or until golden.

4. Then, flip and continue to bake for an additional 10 minutes or until crispy on the bottom of the wings.

5. Remove and serve immediately.

Big Game Hot Wings

Be a big fan of these wings. You can actually prepare the sauce in advance and freeze it. You can adjust the sweetness and heat as you like.

Servings: 10

Cook time: 2 hours and 45 minutes

Ingredients:

- 2/3 c. Prepared Yellow Mustard
- 3 ¾ tbsp. Ketchup
- 2 c. Water
- ½ c. Distilled White Vinegar
- 1 c. White Sugar, Or to Taste
- 7 tbsp. Hot Pepper Sauce or To Taste
- 1 ½ tsp. Crushed Red Pepper Flakes
- 2 lb. Chicken Wings and Drumettes
- 1 Orange, Peel and Pith Removed, Chopped

Instructions:

1. In a heavy saucepan, boil crushed red pepper flakes, hot pepper sauce, sugar, vinegar, and water over medium heat.

2. Mix ketchup and yellow mustard into the sauce.

3. Next, mix in orange. Boil the sauce again, lower the heat, and simmer for 2-4 hours until thickened.

4. Then, set your oven to 350°F (175°C) to preheat.

5. In a big baking sheet, put the chicken wings.

6. Bake approximately for 30-45 minutes in the preheated oven until the inside is not pink anymore and the wings turn brown.

7. Mix into the sauce with the baked wings and enjoy.

Caramelized Chicken Wings

You can use both electric frying pan and stove top to prepare this recipe. It is a very delicious meal you will enjoy.

Servings: 6

Cook time: 1 hour and 5 minutes

Ingredients:

- 1 c. Water
- ½ c. White Sugar
- 1/3 c. Soy Sauce
- 2 tbsp. Peanut Butter
- 1 tbsp. Honey
- 2 tsp. Wine Vinegar
- 1 tbsp. Minced Garlic
- 12 Chicken Wings, cut off the tips and the wings at half joint
- 1 tsp. Sesame Seeds, Or to Taste (Optional)

Instructions:

1. Combine garlic, wine vinegar, honey, peanut butter, soy sauce, sugar, and water in a big frying pan or an electric frying pan until smooth and the sugar dissolves.

2. Add the wings to the sauce, put a cover on and simmer, 30 minutes. Remove the cover, then simmer for another 30 minutes until the sauce is thick and the wings are soft; baste the wings with the sauce sometimes.

3. Sprinkle sesame seeds over.

Bombay Chicken Wings

Chicken wings with a mild curry taste that make a good snack, an appetizer or a game-day treat.

Servings: 6

Cook time: 1 hour and 35 minutes

Ingredients:

- 24 Chicken Wings
- 2 tbsp. Vegetable Oil
- 2 tbsp. Soy Sauce
- 2 tbsp. Minced Green Onion
- 2 Cloves Garlic, Minced
- 1 tsp. Curry Powder
- ½ tsp. Ground Turmeric
- 1/8 tsp. Ground Black Pepper

Instructions:

1. In the resealable plastic bag, mix the black pepper, turmeric, curry powder, garlic, green onion, soy sauce, vegetable oil and chicken wings. Squeeze out air, seal the bag, and keep in the refrigerator no less than 60 minutes.

2. Next, preheat the oven to 175 degrees C (350 degrees F).

3. Spread the chicken wings into the big baking dish.

4. Lastly, bake in preheated oven approximately 25 minutes till the wings become brown.

Chicken Wings with Spicy Apricot Sauce

Flavorful sweet-and-sour sauce for a delicious appetizer. Easy and quick to prepare.

Servings: 6 dozen

Cook time: 25 minutes

Ingredients:

- 3 Dozen Whole Chicken Wings
- 1 ½ c. Cornstarch
- 1 tbsp. Baking Powder
- 1 ½ tsp. Salt
- ½ tsp. Pepper
- ½ tsp. Sugar
- 3 Eggs, Beaten
- Oil for Deep-Fat Frying

Sauce:

- 1 c. (3 Oz.) Dried Apricots
- 1 ¼ c. Water
- 2 tbsp. Sugar
- 2 tbsp. Cider Vinegar
- 2 tbsp. Honey
- ¼ tsp. Cayenne Pepper

Instructions:

1. Cut chicken wings into 3 parts; remove the wing tip part. In a large resealable plastic bag or shallow bowl, combine sugar, pepper, salt, baking powder, and cornstarch. First, dip the chicken pieces in eggs, then generously coat with the cornstarch mixture.

2. Heat oil to 350° in a deep-fat fryer or an electric skillet. Fry the chicken wings set by set until juices run clear, for about 9 minutes. Drain on paper towels and keep warm.

3. In the meantime, combine water and apricots in a large saucepan; bring to a boil. Lower the heat; simmer, covered, until the apricots are softened.

4. Transfer to a food processor or blender. Add cayenne, honey, vinegar, and sugar, process until smooth on high. Cool slightly. Enjoy with the chicken wings.

Breaded Chicken Wings

The coating for these tender wings is made with onion, garlic, and basil. It's very tasty.

Servings: 6-8

Cook time: 45 minutes

Ingredients:

- 2/3 c. Dry Breadcrumbs
- 1 tsp. Onion Powder
- 1 tsp. Dried Basil
- ½ tsp. Garlic Salt
- ½ tsp. Paprika
- 1 Large Egg
- 1 tbsp. Water
- 10 Whole Chicken Wings

Instructions:

1. Mix paprika, garlic salt, basil, onion powder, and breadcrumbs together in a big resealable plastic bag. Stir together water and egg in a small bowl.

2. Slice chicken wings into 3 portions; dispose of the wingtips. In the egg, dip the wings, and then put in the bag and shake to coat.

3. Put in an oil-coated 15x10x1-inch baking pan. Bake at 425° until the juices run clear, about 30-35 minutes, flipping 1 time.

4. Serve and Enjoy!!

Chicken Wings Fricassee

These wings are very flavorful. They are great for dinner.

Servings: 4

Cook time: 1 hour and 5 minutes

Ingredients:

- 12 chicken wings (about 2 ½ lbs.)
- ½ c. all-purpose flour
- 1 tsp. seasoned salt
- ¾ tsp. pepper, divided
- 3 tbsp. vegetable oil
- 2 medium onions, chopped
- 1 garlic clove, minced
- 1 ¼ c. water
- 1 tsp. salt
- Cooked Rice

Instructions:

1. Slice chicken wings into 3 portions; dispose the wing tips. Mix 1/2 teaspoon pepper, seasoned salt, and flour together in a bowl or a resealable plastic bag.

2. Add the wings, mix to evenly coat. Brown all sides of the wings with oil in a big frying pan. Add garlic and onions; cook until soft.

3. Mix in the leftover pepper, salt, and water; stir thoroughly. Boil it, lower the heat. Simmer without a cover until the chicken juices run clear, about 30-35 minutes.

4. Enjoy with rice.

Buttery Hot Wings

These delicious wings have been texture-tested and accepted by a squad of starving firefighters. I hope you'll love them as much as they do!

Servings: 3 dozen (2 cups of sauce)

Cook time: 30 minutes

Ingredients:

- 20 whole chicken wings (4 lb.)
- 2 c. whole wheat flour
- 1 c. all-purpose flour
- 1 tsp. salt
- 1 tsp. paprika
- ¼ tsp. cayenne pepper
- Oil for deep-fat frying

Sauce:

- 1 ½ c. butter, cubed
- 1/3 c. hot pepper sauce
- 3 tbsp. brown sugar
- 2 tbsp. chili sauce
- 2 tbsp. honey
- 1 tbsp. balsamic vinegar
- ¾ tsp. salt
- ¾ tsp. paprika
- ½ tsp. cayenne pepper

Instructions:

1. Cut chicken wings into 3 parts; remove the wing tip parts. Combine cayenne, paprika, salt, and flours in a large resealable plastic bag. Put in the wings, a few at a time, then shake well to coat.

2. Heat 1 in. of oil to 375° in your deep-fat fryer or electric skillet. Fry 6-8 wings at a time until juices run clear, for 3-4 minutes on each side; add more oil if necessary. Drain on paper towels. Move them to a large bowl and keep warm.

3. Combine the sauce ingredients in a large saucepan. Cook and stir over medium heat approximately for 10 minutes until butter is melted. Then, pour over the chicken wings and toss to coat. Serve immediately.

Candied Garlic Chicken Wings

These wings are sticky and sweet like candy!

Servings: 4

Cook time: 1 hour and 15 minutes

Ingredients:

- 1 ½ c. Honey
- 6 tbsp. Soy Sauce
- 2 Cloves Garlic, Minced
- 2 lb. Chicken Wings

Instructions:

1. In a saucepan, heat garlic, soy sauce and honey until boiling.

2. Place the wings in the 9x13-inch baking pan, Add honey mixture over chicken. Wrap in foil and place in refrigerator to marinate for a few hours or up to overnight.

3. Cover and bake for 60 minutes at 375°F (190°C); after 30 minutes, flip wings. Discard foil cover, and then bake for about 15 minutes. Bring wings out of sauce. Bake for 10 minutes on rack. Flip chicken wings. Cook for another 10 minutes.

Sweet Chili Wings

This recipe is super simple to prepare. Very delicious and healthy for any person.

Servings: 5

Cook time: 1 hour and 5 minutes

Ingredients:

- 2 ½ lb. Chicken Wings
- ¾ c. Sweet Chili Sauce (Choose Your Favorite Brand)
- Cooking Oil

Instructions:

1. Preheat your oven to 350 degrees F.

2. Place wings in a lightly greased baking pan. Lightly brush with cooking oil.

3. Bake for about 45-60 minutes. Turning 2 to 3 times while baking.

4. Next, remove from oven.

5. Using tongs dip wings in the sweet chili sauce.

6. Place the wings back in the pan and return to oven for 3-5 minutes.

7. Remove from oven.

8. Lastly, dip the wings in the sauce once more and place on a serving platter.

John's Honey and Spice Wings

Taste the sweet and spicy intoxicating flavor in one dish.

Servings: 7

Cook time: 1 hour and 15 minutes

Ingredients:

- 3 lb. chicken wings
- 1/3 c. Mustard- either Honey Dijon or Honey Mustard
- 1/3 c. hot sauce
- ½ c. honey

Instructions:

1. Preheat oven to 350 degrees F.

2. Place wings in a foil lined pan into the preheated oven. Bake for 45-60 minutes, turning once.

3. As the wings are getting close to done - Mix the honey, hot sauce and mustard, then warm in a saucepan on the stove.

4. Carefully remove the wings from the oven and dip in the warm sauce.

5. Place dipped wings on a serving platter.

Pearl's Russian Wings

This recipe would let you taste the difference of Russian and Soviet dish to other recipes.

Servings: 6

Cook time: 1 hour and 15 minutes

Ingredients:

- 2 lb. Chicken Wings
- 8 oz. Jar Apricot Preserves
- 8 oz. Bottle Red Russian Dressing
- 1 pkg. Dry Onion Soup Mix
- Cooking Oil to Brush Wings Before Baking

Instructions:

1. Preheat oven to 350 degrees F.

2. Place wings in a greased baking pan and lightly brush with oil.

3. Cover and bake for about 45 minutes.

4. While wings are in oven mix Russian dressing and apricot preserves in a saucepan. Warm on low for several minutes. Once the mixture is thoroughly warm add in the dry soup mix, stirring constantly to blend. Keep the mixture warm on the stove.

5. Remove baked wings in pan from oven.

6. Brush the mixture thoroughly on the wings.

7. Return the pan to the oven. Then, bake uncovered for another 7-10 minutes.

8. Remove from oven.

9. Brush wings once more with the mixture and place on a serving dish.

Conclusion

Chicken wings are incredibly great. They are most sought after at the appetizer buffet and as a special game-day menu. If you think, however, the chicken wings are merely game-day treats, you are mistaken. There are lots of chicken wing recipes that you can try at home and serve not just for snacks but also for lunch or dinner. Just like other chicken parts, this choice cut can be boiled, braised, stir-fried, steamed, and more. Although baking and deep frying are common, you can easily use different cooking techniques to create delicious chicken wings recipes, alright.

The hot sauce used for chicken wings is now used with chicken fingers, chicken fries, chicken nuggets, popcorn chicken, shrimp, pizza, spaghetti and so on. Chicken wings are not only served with the hot sauce (although it is considered the traditional variant). Indeed, they can be served with a variety of different sauces such as barbecue sauce, lemon and pepper sauce, with Parmesan, garlic sauce, sweet and sour flavor, honey and mustard sauce, Thai chill, Caribbean jerk, honey and garlic, peanut butter and jelly sauce and many more.

That's what this chicken wing cookbook has proven. We have 60 of the most delightful recipes that you can make at home. While some of them mimic restaurant favorites and the common order at pubs, the rest seem like ordinary family meals. Cook your chicken wings in different ways, and for sure, you will get loud applauds at the dining table. Our chicken wing recipes can easily transform from being game-day treats into family meal favorites in one go.

I hope this book guided you and helped you prepare for the all-time fave food, Chicken Wings. Thank you for reaching the end, and if you have liked this book, please share it with your friends, family and acquaintances.

About the Author

Angel Burns learned to cook when she worked in the local seafood restaurant near her home in Hyannis Port in Massachusetts as a teenager. The head chef took Angel under his wing and taught the young woman the tricks of the trade for cooking seafood. The skills she had learned at a young age helped her get accepted into Boston University's Culinary Program where she also minored in business administration.

Summers off from school meant working at the same restaurant but when Angel's mentor and friend retired as head chef, she took over after graduation and created classic and new dishes that delighted the diners. The restaurant flourished under Angel's culinary creativity and one customer developed more than an appreciation for Angel's food. Several months after taking over the position, the young woman met her future husband at work and they have been inseparable ever since. They still live in Hyannis Port with their two children and a cocker spaniel named Buddy.

Angel Burns turned her passion for cooking and her business acumen into a thriving e-book business. She has authored several successful books on cooking different types of dishes using simple ingredients for novices and experienced chefs alike. She is still head chef in Hyannis Port and says she will probably never leave!

Author's Afterthoughts

With so many books out there to choose from, I want to thank you for choosing this one and taking precious time out of your life to buy and read my work. Readers like you are the reason I take such passion in creating these books.

It is with gratitude and humility that I express how honored I am to become a part of your life and I hope that you take the same pleasure in reading this book as I did in writing it.

Can I ask one small favour? I ask that you write an honest and open review on Amazon of what you thought of the book. This will help other readers make an informed choice on whether to buy this book.

My sincerest thanks,

Angel Burns

If you want to be the first to know about news, new books, events and giveaways, subscribe to my newsletter by clicking the link below

https://angel-burns.gr8.com

or Scan QR-code